SALISBURY

IN OLD PHOTOGRAPHS

A SECOND SELECTION

To my daughter Satu and the handicapped children of Salisbury who will benefit from the sale of this book.

SALISBURY
IN OLD PHOTOGRAPHS
A SECOND SELECTION

COLLECTED BY
PETER DANIELS

Budding
BOOKS

A Budding Book

First published in 1988 by Alan Sutton Publishing Limited

This edition published in 1998 by Budding Books,
an imprint of Sutton Publishing Limited
Phoenix Mill · Thrupp · Stroud · Gloucestershire GL5 2BU

Copyright © Peter R. Daniels, 1988

A catalogue record for this book is available from the British Library

ISBN 1-84015-073-4

Typesetting and origination by
Sutton Publishing Limited.
Printed in Great Britain by
WBC Limited, Bridgend, Mid-Glamorgan.

CONTENTS

INTRODUCTION

Photography is for everyone and, as a hobby, it is more popular now than at any time before. It takes just a fraction of a second for a camera to record an image on film which, when printed, produces a picture that could last for hundreds of years. In fact, a number of photographs taken over a century ago are reproduced in this book which is published at a rather appropriate time. The negative/positive photographic process was invented 150 years ago by William Henry Fox Talbot at Lacock House in Wiltshire. He introduced his 'Calotype' process to the Royal Society on 31 January 1839 in a paper entitled 'Some Account of the Art of Photogenic Drawing'. He experimented with the process continually until 1843 when, after four years of methodical work, he was capable of producing paper images of an acceptable and consistent standard. The Calotype method was soon superseded, however, when in 1851 Frederick Scott Archer introduced the 'wet collodian plate' system and, during the decade that followed, this was the process most widely adopted by the pioneering photographists (photographic artists).

In Salisbury, the first professional photographer was Henry Brooks who set up a 'daylight studio' at 60 High Street in 1858. Initially, like the majority of early photographists, he concentrated on portraiture, producing board-mounted like-nesses in two formats; the 'carte-de-visite' (visiting card size and often used for that purpose) and the 'cabinet print' which was about 4¼ins. × 6½ins. Relative to the number of surviving examples, incalculable quantities of these were produced. The Victorians were fascinated by photographs; they were in fashion and the demand for reproductions of local views, landscapes and events was phenomenal. Photography was here to stay.

Fortunately for us, Salisbury was favoured by many photographers who attempted to establish portrait studios here in the early years. A few disappeared almost as quickly as they came. Others were more successful and continued to provide a useful service well into the twentieth century. The quality and content of their work varied immensely but nevertheless they all contributed something to the visual record of the life and times of the city, its people and their environment. Only a very tiny part of their print output has survived the years and many old photographs have yet to be discovered hidden away in picture albums, cupboards and attics. A representative selection from those that have been uncovered is reproduced in this book.

The photographs are arranged in seven sections and cover the period from the second half of the last century through to the first half of the present. Sections one and seven are concerned with people and, naturally, the initial pictures depict the city's future, its children. They are seen dressed in fancy costumes for the Coronation processions of 1902 and 1911 and in everyday attire as they played in the streets near their homes. Their parents worked hard and whatever free time they had was used to good advantage; many of their recreation activities have been featured under the 'Leisure' heading.

The Market Place is the heart of New Sarum and since the thirteenth century people have gathered there for mass celebrations or to buy and sell provisions and livestock. The second group of photographs recreate the bygone atmosphere of this ancient square. If the Market Place is the heart of the city, then the businesses are the lifeblood and the pictures under 'Trades and Service' show how the people earned their money and where they spent it.

The 'Street and Buildings' section contains almost fifty photographs which were selected mainly from those held in private collections. The majority have not previously been published so there will be a few surprises for even the most avid collector of old photographs. The growing number of transport enthusiasts should appreciate the selection of pictures in section six, many firsts are shown, including Salisbury's first motor cars, buses and delivery vehicles.

The only pictures to appear chronologically are those that illustrate many of the memorable events that took place in Salisbury between 1887 and 1953. The grand public rejoicings and the terrible disasters which were observed by our ancestors can now be experienced again by us, in a way only made possible through the medium of photography. Many of you may now be stimulated into looking out your own old family pictures and, for this reason, I have included here a list of early Salisbury photographers. The information can be used to establish the approximate date of old photographs which carry the photographer's name. The data is as accurate as present-known sources of reference allow.

SECTION ONE

People

YOUNG ROBBIE KEY, in the middle of the picture, turned on the Christmas Tree lights in the cathedral in 1949. The picture was taken by Henry Wills for the *Salisbury Journal*. Robert Key is now our Member of Parliament.

THOUSANDS OF SCHOOL CHILDREN took part in a procession to celebrate the coronation of Edward VII on Friday, 18 July 1902. This is the Brown Street Baptist Church float, representing Spring.

THE CORONATION OF GEORGE V was celebrated in much the same manner. The procession and fete, held for the young, took place on 23 June 1911. St Martin's School children adopted a country theme for their cart.

Photographers frequently used children to bring their pictures to life and these youngsters in the High Street look quite pleased with the idea of improving this view of 1916.

THESE CHILDREN in Fair View Road show us that head wear was very much in fashion in 1912.

A YOUNG MAN rests for a while before proceeding with his hand-cart along Hulse Road in 1910. The baskets contained fresh vegetables.

GODOLPHIN SCHOOL GIRLS joined the crowds in the Market Place in 1910 to hear the proclamation of the accession to the throne of George V. Miss Street can be seen just left of centre, under the hat with the plain band.

'DRINK LIKE A FISH, WATER ONLY' was the message that members of the temperance movement projected during a Band of Hope meeting at Victoria Park in June 1908.

CHILDREN AT THE OCTOBER FAIR. The Galloping Horses ride was driven by a steam engine.

CARAVAN MISSIONS were common right up to the Second World War and this particular one was photographed by Harold Whitworth around 1922. The preacher is seen sitting at the pedal organ.

CHILDREN AT VICTORIA PARK IN 1900. The thatched rustic shelter is sadly no longer there.

PEACE AND QUIET for the young and old at Riverside Walk in 1907. The little girl with the pram was not concerned about the camera, she was more interested in what her friend was picking up.

BOYS FROM THE YMCA SWIMMING CLUB at the Rollestone Street Baths in 1908. The caretakers were, believe it or not, Mr and Mrs Poole. Horace Messer, photographer and YMCA secretary, is standing at the back, sporting a beard.

A SWIMMING SESSION for boys only at the open pool behind the Town Mill in 1907. The water was drawn directly from the River Avon.

ST MARK'S SCHOOL SPORTS DAY around 1910. The picture proves that all sports days were not wet: these spectators were using umbrellas to shelter from the sun.

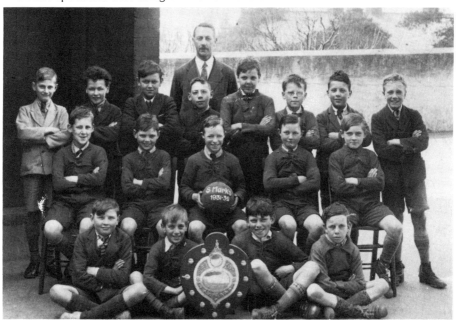

ST MARK'S FOOTBALL TEAM won the Elementary Schools Football League in 1931. Their headmaster was Edward Charles Scott.

FRANK KERLEY, this little girl's grandfather, was one of the men who manoeuvered the Giant around the town between 1893 and 1902. Our picture shows two-year-old Kathleen with her mother, Rosa.

KATHLEEN wearing fashions of the late twenties. The picture was taken by E. Macy.

THOMAS OGDEN STEVENS was born in 1800. He was Mayor of Salisbury in 1828 when photography had yet to be introduced. He lived to be 84 years of age.

FREDERICK GRIFFIN was mayor at the time of Queen Victoria's Golden Jubilee in 1887. He was proprietor of a coal and timber stores in Fisherton Street. Recently, a painting of him wearing his mayoral robes was restored and hung in the Guildhall.

TWO OF THE GROTESQUE CHARACTERS that toured the city streets to celebrate the Golden Jubilee of Queen Victoria on Wednesday, 22 June 1887.

ON THE EVENING OF THE NEXT DAY a multitude of children gathered on the Greencroft where they were entertained by these weird characters in their colourful costumes. In the midst of the crowd were masked men wearing large noses, imps, demons, monkeys and even a dame or two. Surely some of the children found them frightening.

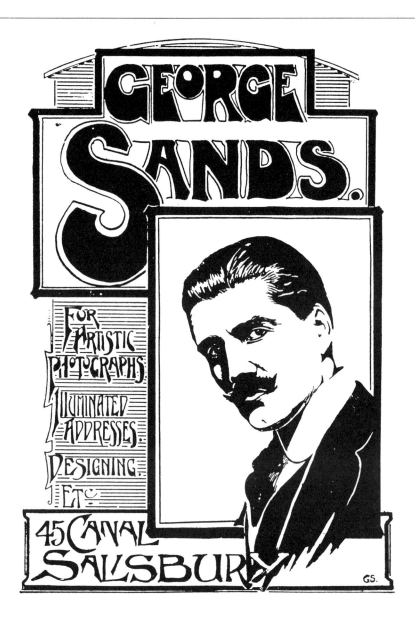

The Market Place

THE MARKET PLACE on a sunny day in 1906. Whitfield Cosser, a Castle Street photographer, took this picture.

THE MARKET PLACE around 1878, taken from a first-floor window of John Ilsley's Gun Shop, now Thomas Cook Travel. The railings around the Council Chamber have disappeared.

THE SYDNEY HERBERT STATUE, which now stands in Victoria Park, was unveiled on 29 June 1863. Herbert was Minister of War during the Crimean War and a great friend of Florence Nightingale.

AN EDWARDIAN VIEW OF THE COUNCIL CHAMBER which was built from funds generously provided by Lord Radnor. It was opened on 23 September 1795. The City Fire Brigade parked their wheeled escape ladder there for many years because the fire station was too small to house it.

ON EMPIRE DAY, 24 May 1916, a large crowd assembled near the Council Chamber, and right up front, keeping an eye on the proceedings, was the Chief Constable, Mr Frank Richardson. He was a proud man who liked to be seen.

A TUESDAY MARKET around 1900. Woolley and Wallis' auctioneers' booth can be seen near the arena in the foreground. The firm held weekly sales of Fat, Store and Dead Stock, and on this occasion mainly sheep were being sold.

A SATURDAY MARKET scene in the late 1920s. The trees along Oatmeal Row did not, as now, obscure the view of the buildings.

HAND-MADE GOODS of every description were displayed at this particular market in 1906. The table on the left was covered with tiny wicker containers and beyond was a stall selling fruit and vegetables. To the right, large wicker baskets were being shown and nearest the camera on that side was a meat stall.

THE HENRY FAWCETT STATUE looks out over Blue Boar Row from its position in the Market Place. When Whitfield Cosser captured this scene in 1904 he had not yet moved to Salisbury.

A SUNNY TUESDAY AFTERNOON IN 1916. John Jeffery & Son, the auctioneers from Donhead St Mary, were conducting their weekly sale of sheep.

A TUESDAY MARKET in 1906. Everyone seems so unhurried and the only obvious movement was that of a woman trying to manoeuvre her hand-cart through the crowds.

A VERY BUSY MARKET DAY SCENE in the 1920s. The trestled cages, lined up along the bottom right of the picture, contained live poultry. Behind them several horse-drawn wagons stood waiting to be unloaded.

A MORE LEISURELY ATMOSPHERE at this market in 1906. The chap bending down in the middle of the picture was asking for trouble: behind him was a cow with a real glint in its eye.

ANDERTON AND ROWLAND were regular providers of thrills and spills at the Salisbury October Fairs. In this 1927 picture their Noah's Arc ride is positioned between two sets of galloping horses.

AT THIS OCTOBER FAIR, just before the First World War, all the old favourites are featured. The Swinging Boats and the Helter Skelter are to the right and on the left can be seen the Galloping Horses, the Scenic Railway and Marshall Hill's Colourful Cars. The most daring rides cost just one penny.

FOR WAR BOND WEEK in March 1918 a battle tank came to town to highlight the event. The noisy metal monster is seen leaving the Market Place to begin a tour of the streets.

SEVERAL HUNDRED SOLDIERS paraded in the Market Place to observe Empire Day on Friday, 24 May 1918.

THE LAST PUBLIC DINNER to be held in the Market Place was for the coronation of George V in June 1911. The picture above shows Mayor Richard Wilson, Mr Locker-Lampson MP and several representatives of the church at the high table.

THE GIANT provides an interesting centrepiece for this group photograph of some willing helpers at the 1911 public dinner. A few thousand pints of beer were drunk that day and it looks as if the chap with the watering can is waiting for his turn to fill up from the barrel.

QUEEN VICTORIA'S GOLDEN JUBILEE. 3500 men sat down to a public dinner in the Market Place. They consumed nearly 2½ tons of meat, 25 gallons of bread and 1500 pounds of plum pudding. All washed down with 20 barrels of ale and 1800 bottles of ginger pop. A special plate was designed by Copelands which displayed the words 'City of Salisbury. Victoria Jubilee 1837–1887'. These plates are occasionally seen at auctions and antique markets.

COUNTRY BUSES LINED UP IN FRONT OF THE COUNCIL CHAMBER in the winter of 1921. They came from Amesbury, Broughton, Chilmark, Handley, Landford and Shrewton. There were a few horse-drawn buses in the Market Place too and at least one traction engine: its column of steam can be seen rising through the trees.

ANOTHER VIEW OF THE COUNTRY BUSES, taken on the same day. To the left is the Royal Red from Shaftesbury and to the right the vans belonging to Ranger of Durrington, Sainsbury of Shrewton, Knight of Winterslow and White of Netheravon. The horse-drawn van belonged to Parson Brothers of Winterslow who later operated a converted London General omnibus.

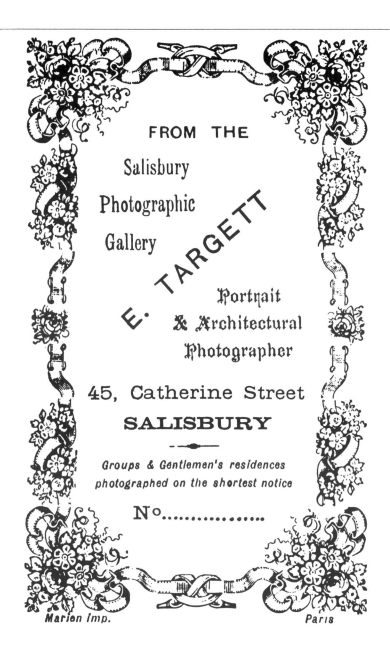

FROM THE

Salisbury

Photographic

Gallery

E. TARGETT

Portrait
& Architectural
Photographer

45, Catherine Street

SALISBURY

*Groups & Gentlemen's residences
photographed on the shortest notice*

N°..................

Marion Imp.

Paris

SECTION THREE

Streets and Buildings

CASTLE STREET IN 1905, by Whitfield Cosser. Milford House, the ivy-covered building on the left, was the home of Richard Dear, a wine and spirit merchant.

A LATE NINETEENTH-CENTURY VIEW OF THE CATHEDRAL from the Bishop's Palace. The picture was taken by Francis George Osborn Stuart who has left us a fascinating visual record of Salisbury in the last century. Thankfully, much of his work survives in museums and private collections.

BISHOP ALLAN BEECHER WEBB and his family relaxing in the grounds of the Deanery before 1907. The gardener was taking a break from cutting the grass; perhaps he wanted to ensure that his image was clear in the picture.

THE WEST FRONT OF THE DEANERY, 1905. The gardener is seen sweeping the paths with a besom, a tool that is not used too often these days.

PUPILS OUTSIDE THE CHORISTERS SCHOOL IN 1902. One of many picture postcards that the boys used to keep in touch with their friends and relatives.

THE BISHOP'S SCHOOL IN 1905. The message on this postcard reads, 'Hope you have not this picture already, two new girls started today, one is weekly. My love to Granny and Granpa. From Dot, Friary House.'

THE HIGH STREET GATE IN 1905, showing the statue of King Edward VII. On many early pictures it was referred to as the North Gate. The grey-bearded gentleman was passing the College of Matrons.

ST ANN'S GATE during the First World War. Frank Simmonds' horse-drawn pantechnicon was parked inside the Close, delivering a piece of furniture which had been purchased from his showroom in Catherine Street.

THE HIGH STREET towards the end of the last century, another of the F.G.O. Stuart views. On the right, at Edwin Macy's Art Repository and Fancy Goods Shop, a sign advertises local views. Some of the photographs used in this album came from there. When this picture was taken, the shop between Macy and the Old George Hotel was vacant, but it was soon leased to Frederick Cowmeadow who set up a drapery store there.

THE HIGH STREET IN 1908 when there were goods and services to satisfy most people. Thirty-five different trades were operated by forty-eight companies.

THE OLD GEORGE HOTEL in the mid-thirties. The upper storeys have changed very little, but the façade at street level has been removed to form an entrance to the Old George Mall shopping precinct.

CRANE STREET AROUND 1890. A few yards down the street on the south side, at number 87, Sydney Briant ran a bakery. He was well established there by the turn of the century when he moved to 9 Castle Street.

FISHERTON MILL ROAD was completely tranformed after the severe rain storms of early January 1915. For a number of days boats and carts were the most practical forms of transport.

DEWS ROAD IN 1913. In the distance is the Salisbury Times Printing Works and, nearest the camera, Henry Buckle's health food shop; his daughter is leaning on the window frame. Henry Buckle took hundreds of street photographs including the one reproduced above.

AN EDWARDIAN VIEW OF THE WESLEYAN CHURCH in Wilton Road. The wall and railings were removed some years ago.

WILTON AND DEVIZES ROADS IN 1905. At the junction was Portland House, the ivy-covered residence of photographer Theodore Brown. He moved to Castle Street in 1902 where he earned fame as an inventor of stereoscopic adaptors for cameras.

THE ANGEL HOTEL at 66 Fisherton Street, around 1907. An advertisement of the time read: 'First class family and commercial; nearest to station and close to cathedral; electric light throughout; motor garage and stabling; moderate tarriff; omnibus meets most trains; Tel, 111.'

THE SUMMERLOCK BRIDGE AREA of Fisherton Street in 1915. The building now occupied by Yorkshire Fisheries was covered with posters, including one for the Palace Theatre.

FISHERTON STREET after the record snowstorm of 25 April 1908. Mr Futcher braved the cold for a few minutes to record this unusual scene; his studio is the third building on the left.

THE COUNTY HOTEL IN 1906 was the largest first-class family hotel in Wiltshire and it was highly recommended by the AA. Miss Jordan, the manageress for a number of years, always offered a warm welcome to the visiting motorist.

THE FISHTERTON CLOCK TOWER IN 1915. The little building to the right was erected for the convenience of the cab drivers who waited for fares outside the Infirmary.

A FUNERAL CORTÈGE IN BRIDGE STREET C.1907. The pedestrians were most likely pursuing their everyday activities rather than being there to observe the procession.

SILVER STREET IN 1915, where David Stevens, the draper and outfitter, occupied numbers 55–59 which were known collectively as Salisbury House. At the High Street junction (Snook's Corner) William Snook had his butchery shop.

THE LADS TO THE LEFT seem more intrigued by the photographer than the early motor car that was passing the Poultry Cross in 1906. Outside Lipton's store, Sutton's cart was being loaded. The local agent for that firm was the Mayor, Mr Frank Baker.

THE POULTRY CROSS on a market day in 1935.

THE POULTRY CROSS AND SILVER STREET around 1870. Soon after the picture was taken, Richardson Brothers, the wine and spirit merchants, had a new building constructed on the corner of High Street and Bridge Street, where Barclays Bank is now.

FISH MARKET AND BUTCHER ROW, 1903. The Wheatsheaf Inn was at 7 Fish Market where George Brown was the proprietor. At number 9 Priscilla Hart was in business. William Snook was on the opposite corner in Butcher Row and a little way along from there, at number 15, was George Coombs' Victoria Coffee Tavern.

THE CHURCH OF ST THOMAS OF CANTERBURY IN 1900. The picture postcard could still be purchased from newsagents in the 1930s.

THE MARKET HOUSE, 1906. It was officially opened on 24 May 1859. The building was designed by Mr Strapp of the South Western Railway who specified Bath stone for the façade.

A SOLID-TYRED WILTS & DORSET BUS leaving Blue Boar Row at Sly's Corner *en route* to Bournemouth via Ringwood, early in 1921.

THE LIVERPOOL, LONDON & GLOBE INSURANCE OFFICES at 21 Queen Street, c.1920. The building, which was formerly a Wilts & Dorset Bank, is now occupied by the Job Centre and the Hungerford Wine Company.

WINCHESTER STREET, 1906. On the left, just beyond Goddard the Saddler, was the Coach and Horses Inn managed by Mary Ann Crouch. Howard Harris' carriage building works were on the right and further up the street on that side were the cycle depots of Charles Langford and Alfred Asbridge.

QUEEN STREET, 1905. The best known establishment at that time was the Turkish Baths, owned by the Jenkins family.

MILFORD STREET, 1900. The perspective was distorted by the camera, giving an impression of great width. This street was not often photographed and very few early pictures survive.

ST ANN STREET AND ST MARTIN'S CHURCH STREET, before 1936. The terraced houses and the Beckingsale Training Home for Girls, formerly known as Moorlands, were demolished when Churchill Way was constructed.

ST ANN STREET, 1916. The woman on the left was probably looking to see what bargains were on display in William Prince's shop window.

THE ROSE AND CROWN at East Harnham in 1911, when William Preston was manager. The visitors who travelled by car could fill up from the manual petrol pump and the posters to the right advertised the *Salisbury Times*, popular songs and Salisbury Races.

THE OLD MILL FORD at West Harnham, 1925. Frederick Sutton's Ford Model T bread van was parked outside the Three Crowns public house.

SALISBURY RACES before July 1908. This picture is reproduced from a Whitfield Cosser postcard on which Edward Hibberd wrote a message: 'What do you think of our racecourse? I am caretaker here.'

WILTON ROAD IN 1907. The people, passing the Half Way House Hotel, were returning from a day at the races. The cheeky young lads were trying to get a free ride on the back of their carriages. They became known as 'Whipper-snappers' and often a passenger could be heard to shout 'Whip behind driver, whip behind.'

CATHERINE STREET IN 1937. A night photograph by F. Futcher of the coronation decorations which were described in the *Salisbury Times* as being the prettiest in the city.

IN DAYLIGHT THE DECORATIONS LOOKED VERY DIFFERENT. The red, white and blue streamers hung from buildings at intervals of a few feet and strings of coloured lights were carried the whole length of the street.

ST JOHN STREET, 1916. This souvenir view of Salisbury was published by Sydney Jefferies, the bookseller, stationer and newsagent of 11 Queen Street. 12 different views were issued.

NUMBER ONE NEW STREET, decorated for the 1911 Coronation. Thomas Miles lived there. He was a carpentry instructor at the Bishop's School and his wife Eliza was a dressmaker. It is now the Wig and Quill Inn.

THE CANAL IN 1906. To the left is Bingham's Corner where William Bingham ran a drapery store and across the road were the Assembly Rooms, now W.H. Smith.

THE CANAL FROM MILFORD STREET IN 1907. Brinsmead's Music shop is to the right and Thomas Bloom's department store to the left. The trees in the distance were cut down many years ago and now coaches and taxis park there.

NELSON ROAD IN 1912. The post office and shop, founded by Roland Chapman around 1909, had served the community well for three generations before closing in May 1984. Scammel's Toll Gate can be seen in the distance.

THE TOLL GATE AND BRIDGE IN NELSON ROAD was established by Thomas Scammel in 1899. The last toll was paid on 22 July 1931 when the gate and bridge were purchased by Salisbury Corporation. This view shows W. Handford passing through on 16 May 1931.

THE SALISBURY TIMES was first published on Saturday, 14 March 1868 and is still going strong.

SECTION FOUR

Events

THE PRESENTATION OF MEDALS in the Market Place on Empire Day 1919. James Macklin was Mayor and on the stage with him was the Durham Light Infantry Band. Men of the 2nd Wiltshire Regiment formed the guard of honour.

THE SHOPS AND PUBLIC BUILDINGS were decorated for the Golden Jubilee of Queen Victoria in June 1887 and one of the most colourful was at 52 Fisherton Street where the Mayor, Mr Frederick Griffin, ran his coal and timber stores. At the top of the façade was a large banner in red and white with the words 'God Bless our Queen' and below that, above the arch, was a transparent portrait of Her Majestry which was illuminated at night much to the delight of the passers-by.

THE BRITANNIA was one of many carnival floats that followed the course of the Jubilee procession around the streets of Salisbury on 22 June 1887 . . .

THE BRITANNIA FLOAT is seen turning from Milford Street into Catherine Street. The people marching before it represented local friendly societies.

JUBILEE DECORATIONS, JUNE 1887. Henry White of the Bull Hotel had an ornamented arch erected in Fisherton Street. The timber-framed structure was covered in evergreen and at night it took on a fairy-like appearance when it was illuminated by gas lamps.

THE MARRIAGE OF THE DUKE OF YORK AND PRINCESS VICTORIA MAY OF TECK (later George V and Queen Mary) was celebrated in Salisbury, 6 July 1893. The Volunteer Fire Brigade commissioned this picture to record the event.

ON THE SAME DAY, the Giant and his mettle-some esquire Hob Nob were photographed with their entourage outside Naish and Son Carriage Building Works. At the back, to the left, with peaked cap and moustache is Frank Kerley.

EDWARD VII'S CORONATION CELEBRATIONS. In the Market Place on Saturday, 9 August 1902 the Salisbury Detachment of the 1st Wilts Volunteer Corps fired a *feu-de-joie* to commence the festivities.

MEMBERS OF THE WOMENS FORESTERS COURT, 'Queen of the Valley' with their float featuring young ladies of Great Britain, America, India, Italy and Japan. They were photographed in front of the triumphal arch at the entrance to Castle Street.

THE SALISBURY CYCLING AND ATHLETIC CLUB led the decorated cars section of the coronation procession. Their theme was national sports and pastimes.

HARRIETT BARTLETT'S FEMALE LODGE OF ODDFELLOWS arranged this carnival float. In the centre was a large palm (lent by Lord Radnor) which was surrounded by a fine selection of pot plants and flowers.

THE OPENING CEREMONY of the new Public Library in Chipper Lane, 2 October 1905. The Mayor, Mr Keith Dowden, and other civic dignitaries attended.

THE NEW FREE LIBRARY, its fine late Gothic character enhanced by the use of white Bath stone. A £4000 donation was made by multi-millionaire Andrew Carnegie.

THE FIRST HOSPITAL CARNIVAL PROCESSION *en route* to Victoria Park, 20 June 1906. Chief Constable Frank Richardson is seen mounted at the head of the parade ...

... THE GOOD SAMARITAN CAR, entered by the Harriett Bartlett Female Lodge of Oddfellows, was awarded first prize and 24 years were to pass before the event was staged again.

THE SALISBURY RAIL DISASTER, 1 July 1906. The crash attracted thousands of sightseers and dozens of photographers who came from all over the country. Many of their pictures were published as postcards like this one from Horace Messer ...

... TWENTY-EIGHT PEOPLE were killed when the express train crashed at the L & SW railway station. Two steam cranes were called in to remove the mass of tangled wreckage.

PRINCESS CHRISTIAN came to Salisbury on 27 November 1906, to open a bazaar at the County Hall in Endless Street. This event was organised to raise money for the YMCA (Winchester Street) building fund . . .

. . . THE PRINCESS went, from the bazaar, to the Infirmary with her companion for the day, Lady Tennant. After a tour of the wards the royal visitor departed in an open carriage.

SALISBURY VOLUNTEER FIRE BRIGADE CAPTAIN, Mr J.M. Folliott presents a silver key, engraved with the City Arms, to the Mayor, Samuel Grove, who officially declared the fire station open, 1 May 1907. The building cost £1700.

THE APPLIANCE BAY, with doors opening into Salt Lane, featured white-glazed brick walls and a parquet floor. The Watch and Duty Rooms were on the Endless Street side.

THE STEAM FIRE ENGINE 'ALERT' rapidly leaving the Fire Station *en route* to the Market Place where water jets were demonstrated to an enthusiastic crowd. Pictures of the demonstration are featured on page 116 of Peter Saunders' volume of *Salisbury in Old Photographs*.

FIREMAN WILLIAM (BILL) MIGGINS. The resident station keeper and the only full-time paid member of staff.

A LIFEBOAT DEMONSTRATION was arranged by Mayor Grove on Wednesday, 7 July 1907. Four powerful horses are seen pulling the craft down Catherine Street on its way to Harnham . . .

. . . THE CAVALCADE eventually reached Harnham Meadows, where, much to the delight of the spectators, the boat was launched. £100 was raised and donated to the RNLI.

THE HEAVIEST SNOWFALL for almost thirty years transformed the Salisbury landscape on 25 April 1908. Only a handful of brave traders set up for the Saturday Market.

'PRETTY CORNER'. On many early photographs the Western end of North Walk in the Close is referred to as 'Pretty Corner' which describes this snow scene perfectly.

THE L & S W STATION looked very festive as the preparations were well advanced for the visit of King Edward VII and Queen Alexandra. 27 June 1908.

THE ROYAL COUPLE make their way down South Western Road *en route* to Wilton House. The King raises his hat to acknowledge the waving crowds . . .

... OUTSIDE ST PAUL'S CHURCH the excited children wait impatiently for the procession to pass. A sign outside the church reads, 'Welcome to the King and Queen' ...

... IN THE WILTON ROAD, at West End, Messrs Saunders had built a mediaeval arch and a mounted policeman is keeping an eye on it.

A SERIOUS FIRE occured at Williamson's Clock Factory in Southampton Road, 27 May 1909, and in a short time it was burnt to the ground. Spectators came from all over the district.

THE DESTRUCTION is vividly portrayed in this picture taken four hours after the height of the blaze. A disaster fund was set up to benefit the 81 employees who lost their jobs and many local firms took on extra workers to lessen their hardship.

THE GIANT, his associates and the Mayor, Richard Wilson, on the occasion of King George V's coronation, 22 June 1911. The picture was taken at Waters and Rawlence's yard near the Market House.

THE FISHERTON CONSERVATIVE CLUB entered their float 'Britannia' in the 1911 coronation procession, seen here passing David Stevens' Salisbury House in Silver Street.

The Mayoress, Mrs Sutton, christened the first Sarum motor fire engine with the customary bottle of wine across the radiator, 29 January 1913. Chief Officer Rawlings looked on as she named the engine 'Fawcett' in honour of a former Brigade Captain . . .

. . . THE MARKET PLACE was ringed with spectators who watched in amazement as the pumping capability of the 'Fawcett' was demonstrated against that of the old steamer 'Alert'.

FISHERTON STREET FLOODED on 5 January 1915. Prolonged and heavy rains fell causing the rivers to overflow and millions of gallons of water poured into Fisherton and the Close ...

... NELSON'S AND PARSONS' at 80 and 82 Fisherton Street were under nearly 14 inches of water. The lady in the picture was given a chair to stand on.

A RECEPTION was given for 180 guests at the Council House, 23 January 1919. Most of the party were returned prisoners of war and Mayor James Macklin presented each man with a silver-plated cigarette case.

PUPILS AND TEACHERS OF ST OSMUND'S SCHOOL marching past the New Theatre in Castle Street during the Children's Peace Pageant, 28 July 1919. They portrayed Domesday at Old Sarum.

THE PRINCE OF WALES was in Salisbury to open the Wiltshire Agricultural Association's annual show at the Butts Fair Field, 24 May 1923. This photograph shows the VIPs on the steps of the Council Chamber.

THE PRINCE then inspected wolf cubs of the 3rd Salisbury pack. To the Prince's right stood Miss Gwendolyn Ellis and Wilfred Chaplin, the Cub and Scout Masters.

THE 700TH ANNIVERSARY OF SALISBURY was celebrated from 27 June to 2 July 1927: This picture shows members of the Leather Workers' Guild, dressed in period costume, ready to take part in the Centenary Procession. The following day, more than 3000 school children participated in their own carnival parade; they toured the city streets in costumes covering seven centuries of Salisbury Schools. The route terminated at Victoria Park in time for the May Day Revels.

THE PUPILS AND TEACHERS OF THE GODOLPHIN SCHOOL in procession along the Canal. Elizabeth Godolphin and her nephew William were followed by groups of schoolgirls, all representing different periods.

MAYOR JOHN HUDSON CROWNED VIOLET BATH as the May Queen at Victoria Park. He is seen presenting her with a silver wand.

THE TOP PRIZE IN THE HOSPITAL CARNIVAL DRAW for 1930 was a Morris Minor Saloon, seen here in Blue Boar Row. John Moore of Oxford bought the winning ticket.

AUNTY SMILER, THE GIANTESS, pushing her pram in Bourne Park just before the Hospital Carnival Parade. She was assembled by the staff of Salisbury Steam Laundry.

'STOP ME AND BUY ONE'. In May 1935 the staff at Walls Ice Cream Depot had their picture taken as a souvenir of King George's Silver Jubilee. Albert Hand, the under manager, is sitting on the chair to the left.

KING GEORGE V'S SILVER JUBILEE DAY, 6 May 1935. The parade included the Minstrel Band of Harnham. Mr Card provided the lorry.

A SERIOUS FIRE destroyed the Co-operative Furnishing Store in Milford Street on Monday, 13 September 1937. The Salisbury Volunteer Fire Brigade responded very quickly and two motor pumps were immediately dispatched. Both experienced difficulty in reaching the blaze, however, because within minutes excited crowds had blocked all approaches to the scene. Damage to the Co-op, Constad's Jewellers and the Cathedral Hotel was estimated at around £15,000.

THE PARENTS OF CHARLES ROAD AND CHARLES STREET raised £42 during Coronation Week in June 1953 to give their children a street party. The children are watching a Punch and Judy show given by Stafford Veal.

A PEACE PROCESSION IN SILVER STEET, just after the Second World War. The marchers represented the Church, Salisbury Corporation and the military forces. Jock Kerley carried the City mace and Mayor Frederick Courtney followed.

FROM THE

Photographic

Studio OF

THEODORE BROWN

Portland House, Fisherton, Salisbury.

Negatives kept. Copies may be had by giving the number

No.............

SECTION FIVE

Trades and Services

SHEEP SHEARING in the barn at Parsonage Farm, Old Sarum, around 1907. Farm hands Albert and William Kerley are in the group.

JENKINS BROTHERS IRONMONGERS on the corner of Endless Street and Winchester Street before 1897 when they had been trading for about 50 years. In 1899 Joseph Edwin Pinder became a director of the company and the name changed to Jenkins and Pinder. The Jenkins name was dropped in 1926 and two further generations of the Pinder family kept the business alive for another 60 years.

JOHN LAMPARD'S EXETER STREET BAKERY IN 1908. His canvas-covered bread van advertised his grocery shop and rope and twine manufacturing business.

FREDERICK SUTTON'S TOBACCONIST, CONFECTIONERY AND RESTAURANT BUSINESS at numbers 11–13 High Street, around 1904. Frederick Sutton is standing next to the shop girls with Joseph James and the Swiss chef on the right.

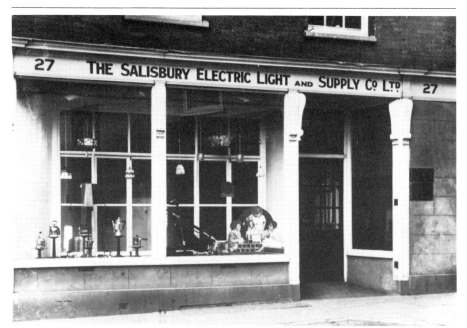

THE SALISBURY ELECTRIC LIGHT AND SUPPLY COMPANY'S SHOP at 27, Market Place in the 1920s. The manager, A.B. Randall, displayed a fascinating selection of early electric vacuum cleaners and tea and coffee pots. Knapman and Bament now occupy this site.

39 BLUE BOAR ROW IN 1887. Frederick Augustus Blake traded there as printer, bookbinder, bookseller, stationer, fancy goods dealer, newsagent and publisher. The shop was demolished a few years later when the Wilts & Dorset Bank was extended.

ERNEST JAMES LONGMAN outside his cycle depot at 97 Fisherton Street in 1911. All the things you would expect were displayed in his window: bells, tyres, lamps, oil, chains and three bicycles.

WILLIAM CRIPP'S SHOP on the corner of Catherine and Milford Streets, around 1910. The business was established in 1783 but the Cripps were not involved until 1857. Can you spot the error?

THE MONUMENTAL MASONRY on the corner of St John and St Ann Streets, in 1897. Millward & Co. purchased the concern from William Osmond in 1890, but his son, Clement Osmond, stayed on and later became manager.

HARDY & SON'S SALESMEN with their traps outside their retail premises at 3–5 Catherine Street, early this century. Cripp's were at number one and James Macklin's Jewellers at seven.

TOM OKE'S STAFF, SHOP AND DELIVERY VAN in Milford Street, just after the Second World War. The Morris van was still in its wartime livery, the wings were edged with white but the headlamp masks had been removed.

HANCOCK'S SHOPPING CENTRE in Oatmeal Row. The shop was overflowing with flags and bunting for the 1937 coronation.

TURNER & BRITTON'S GARAGE at 41–43 Winchester Street in 1927. They were agents for Austin and Daimler. A sign in the window advertised the new Austin Six Saloon at £198. Goddards now have showrooms there.

AN EDWARDIAN FAMILY hired this Renault landaulette from W. Rowland & Sons of Castle Street in 1909. They are probably best remembered, however, for their charabanc outings of the 1920s.

THE SALES AND FACTORY STAFF of the Scout Motor Company, outside their new Eclipse Works in Churchfields Road in 1907. Joseph Percy Dean and Albert and William Burden were the directors. They had been manufacturing engines since 1902.

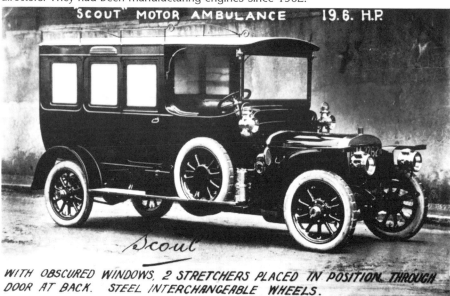

SCOUT MOTOR AMBULANCE 19.6. H.P.

WITH OBSCURED WINDOWS, 2 STRETCHERS PLACED IN POSITION THROUGH DOOR AT BACK. STEEL INTERCHANGEABLE WHEELS.

THE FIRST SCOUT MOTOR AMBULANCE was supplied to the Old Sarum Hospital in 1912. The eye-catching vehicle was finished in dark blue with red highlights and blue leather upholstery. The radiator and lamps were made of brass.

A WINDSOR DAIRY FLOAT around 1904. The proprietor was Henry George Percy of Cowslip Farm off Devizes Road. The cart carried a seventeen-gallon churn which rested on a swinging platform so that it stayed upright. The wooden boxes at each end contained 'Fresh Eggs and Butter'.

THE WILTSHIRE AGRICULTURAL ASSOCIATION held their annual show in the Corporation Fair Field at the Butts, Salisbury, on Tuesday and Wednesday, 23–24 May 1911. Our picture shows a section of the field where the trade stands of Brown & May of Devizes, Scout Motors of Salisbury, Wallis & Stevens of Basingstoke and Reeves & Son of Trowbridge were sited.

JOHN VARLEY ARMITAGE ENGINEERS of St Ann's Foundry also exhibited at the 1911 show. They displayed a wide range of manual and mechanical agricultural implements.

THE SALISBURY SHEEP FAIR was held annually on 15 July, at the Butts. In 1907 about 22,000 animals were penned, and at the auctions held by Waters & Rawlence, the two-teeth ewes were realising an average of 52 shillings per head.

NICHOLAS BROTHERS BAKERY around 1920. Frederick James, one of their skilled confectioners, is operating an electric mixer in the middle of the picture.

WORKERS AT THE MARKET HOUSE taking time out for a group photograph in 1907. The bales of wool were being sealed with needle and twine.

EMPLOYEES OF WORT & WAY BUILDERS on a site before the First World War. The foundations had reached ground level and the bricklayers were preparing to start work.

FREDERICK WILLIAM OCKENDEN with his operatives, repairing a well at Bemerton in 1910. His company sank hundreds of wells throughout southern England and Wales.

OFFICERS OF THE FIRST MUNICIPAL COUNCIL OF GREATER SALISBURY 1904–5. The individual photographs, taken by Horace Messer, were mounted and framed. The original montage is presently displayed in the Guildhall.

COUNCIL WORKERS with their entire stock of 18 heavy horses, at the municipal depot around 1920. The stables can be seen to the right.

THE GENERAL POST OFFICE on the corner of Castle Street and Chipper Lane in 1912. A postman can be seen emptying the postbox on the Castle Street side, his tricycle close by.

THERE WERE NO LONG QUEUES at the General Post Office in the 1920s. You could sit at the oak table and write your postcards in peace and quiet.

THE VOLUNTEER FIRE BRIGADE outside Salt Lane Fire Station in 1936. Mayor Scammel, Alderman Rambridge and Officer Hardy are standing in front of the Dennis fire engine called 'The Chief'. The other appliance, also a Dennis, was named 'The Chairman'.

FIREMAN ALBERT NOYCE wearing his tunic and brass helmet. He also appears in the picture above, standing on 'The Chief' third from the left. Mr Noyce, who is now enjoying his retirement, will be remembered by many as the proprietor of a newsagents shop in Milford Street. Before 1949, the business was operated by Ernest Noyce, his father.

CHRISTMAS AT THE INFIRMARY IN 1924. Mr Futcher took pictures in all the wards and each patient received a free photograph. This is one of them.

THE INFIRMARY. This Whitfield Cosser photograph was published in June 1906 to coincide with the first Hospital Carnival. The cab drivers waited there to pick up passengers.

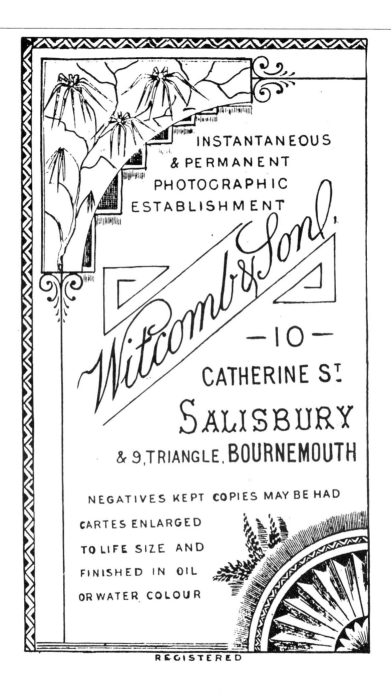

INSTANTANEOUS
& PERMANENT
PHOTOGRAPHIC
ESTABLISHMENT

Witcomb & Son.

—10—

CATHERINE ST.

SALISBURY

& 9, TRIANGLE, BOURNEMOUTH

NEGATIVES KEPT COPIES MAY BE HAD
CARTES ENLARGED
TO LIFE SIZE AND
FINISHED IN OIL
OR WATER COLOUR

REGISTERED

SECTION SIX

Transport

HARDY & SON'S STRAKER STEAM LORRY, decorated for the 1906 Hospital Carnival procession. The photograph was taken by Charles Bridle as the parade passed his hairdressing salon at 67 Fisherton Street.

A HORSE-DRAWN OMNIBUS, early this century. The conductor is seen collecting fares and issuing tickets. The advertisements were for Bloom's sale, Moody & Sons and Moore's footwear.

A PONY AND TRAP. Charles Baxter Sewell and Polly were photographed in the gardens of Moorland House, St Ann Street around 1908.

JOHN LAMPARD'S TWO-HORSE CHARABANCS in Exeter Street, around 1905. Numbers two and three from his fleet are nearest the camera. The family's private car is featured on page 121.

DOCTORS HARCOURT COATES AND SYDNEY ELLIS owned the first car registered in Salisbury. The Scottish-built Paisley Syndicate car was given licence number AM11 in December 1903.

MESSRS STYLE AND GERRISH employed travellers to sell their wares around the neighbouring towns and villages. Driver Fred Shepherd stands proudly by their 1903 Dark Green 10 hp Wolseley.

THE FIRST SCOUT CAR to be sold was in fact the third to be manufactured. It was purchased by Dr William Ord of New Street. His chauffeur is seen with the car soon after it left Burden Bros' Excelsior Works, The Friary, in October 1905.

A STUDEBAKER 15/20 hp five-seater. The dark-blue tourer was licensed as a public service vehicle on 28 May 1915. It was owned by John Charles Lampard of 124 Exeter Street.

JETHRO CRABB, a well-known Salisbury businessman and a lover of motor vehicles, pictured as a young man astride a 1916 Douglas 2½ hp motorbike. He was involved with road transport most of his life. During the First World War he drove taxis and in the twenties he was employed by Sparrow & Vincent as a charabanc driver. Later he restored several vintage cars and was a local committee member of the Veteran Car Club. He died in 1985.

THE FIRST MOTOR VAN registered in Salisbury, indexed AM 764, was owned by Priscilla Hart. The 8–10 hp two-cylinder, 1903 Daimler was supplied by S. & E. Collett of the Castle Street Garage.

A 1906 OVERLAND, purchased second-hand by J.T. Davis & Sons of the Park House Bakery, London Road. The pretty little van, with side display windows, was formerly with the Bristol Steam Oven Works of Fishponds.

BRADSHAW-DESIGNED BELSIZE CARS OF 1921, in the yard behind E.W. Davis & Sons Central Garage at 34 Castle Street. The cars were priced at £275 if fitted with a 9 hp air-cooled engine.

FREDERICK HALLETT ran a taxi business from the Swan Inn at East Harnham. These two landaulettes were in his fleet just after the First World War. The one nearest the camera is a Ford Model T and the other an ex-military Wolseley staff car.

GEORGE MOULD favoured the Ford. The T Model trucks were the backbone of his early fleet. The two dark blue ones shown above were photographed in Brown Street around 1927.

GIBBS MEW & COMPANY'S DARRACQ DRAY, delivering to the White Horse public house at Quidhampton in 1915. They were early users of heavy motor trucks, but not the first; that honour went to Hardy & Son.

A WILTS & DORSET AEC DOUBLE-DECKER, pictured in Bridge Street on its way to Wilton in 1921. The vehicle started work with another operator and carries a Sussex registration number.

HANDSOME HACKNEYS in the Market Place, 1919. Both Scout vehicles were owned by Halls of Orcheston. They regularly ran services between Shrewton, Devizes and Salisbury.

A THORNYCROFT J-TYPE SALOON in the Canal in 1921. It was operated by Salisbury & District Motor Services, the trading name of E.M. Coombes & Company. In the summer of 1914 Ernest Coombes introduced the first daily motor bus service between Amesbury and Salisbury using a 37 hp Scout saloon, but after about twelve weeks the business was sold. In 1919 Coombes set up 'Yellow Victory' and that venture lasted just two years, for soon after this photograph was taken the Wilts & Dorset Motor Service took control.

SPARROW & VINCENT'S DAIMLER CHARABANC. The day-trippers, from the Five Bells in Salt Lane, were off to Weymouth, leaving from the Liverpool, London & Globe offices in Queen Street.

ALFRED WHITE, the Netheravon carrier, regularly parked his GMC van in Castle Street. On this day, in March 1921, a pile of goods was waiting to be loaded for the return journey.

THE ALBION LB41 VAN purchased by Hardy & Son in 1935. W. Goddard & Co. supplied the chassis and the dark green body was fitted at Harry Acton's Coach Works in Greencroft Street.

HARDY & SON'S 1927 MORRIS COMMERCIAL with driver Bill Turner. The photograph was taken by Harry Rewse at the junction of Pembroke Road.

A DAIMLER, A METALURGIQUE AND A SINGER were among eight taxis on private hire to Joseph Groves at The Old Castle Inn about 1911.

THE TAXI RANK in Blue Boar Row, 1921. The first car, a Wolseley, was formerly owned by William Main, the corn merchant. The fourth car, partially hidden by the American landaulette, was the Darracq in which Sidney Spicer was shot dead by deserter Percy Toplis.

LYONS' TEA sent vans to most areas. This one, a Model T Ford, was spotted by Harold Whitworth in 1925. The photograph was taken outside the Roebuck Inn in the Canal.

WALLY GAMBLIN'S AEC MAMMOTH VAN, supplied in 1931 by W. Goddard & Co. The wood and canvas body was hand-built by Tasker of Andover.

TUNNEL JUNCTION, as seen from the London Road in 1906. A Drummond-designed 4-4-0 locomotive is steaming its way out of the tunnel before crossing the points on to the Romsey line.

THE LONDON AND SOUTH WESTERN RAILWAY STATION IN 1906. The cabs always parked in the yard to the left of the picture, pulling forward only when hailed from the station entrance.

A DONKEY CART in Clifton Terrace, around 1906. The people are believed to be members of the Glover family. John Glover was an engine driver. They lived at number 22.

HIGH CLASS PORTRAITS

At Moderate Prices.

◿ ◿ ◿

Wedding and Family Groups taken by appointment.

LOCAL VIEW
POST CARDS

DARK ROOM FOR
AMATEURS.

F. FUTCHER, PHOTOGRAPHER,

19, Fisherton Street, SALISBURY,

Near the Infirmary. |

SECTION SEVEN

Leisure

THE YMCA FOOTBALL TEAM around 1908. The majority of early photographs of Salisbury YMCA events were taken by Horace Messer who was their General Secretary.

LONG BRIDGE IN 1907. The boys' view of the cathedral was little changed from the one experienced by John Constable when he painted his famous masterpiece of Salisbury Cathedral under a rainbow.

DALTON TEBBY with his promenade concert players at the Pavilion, Victoria Park on Whit Monday, 1908. Mr Tebby is seen to the left wearing a boater.

MEMBERS OF THE CHURCH STREET CYCLING CLUB on a day out in 1914.

STAINERS DANCE BAND around 1925. Tommy Stainer is second from the left, between Bill Thurston and Charlie Overton.

THE SWANMORE DANCE BAND founded by Wilfred Marks sometime around 1930. The band lost favour for a while, but was soon reformed as Harry Hand's Swanmore Orchestra.

BASIL GUMMER'S AVON PLAYERS performing *Romeo and Juliet* in the grounds of the Brambles, London Road, in July 1913. The proceeds were given to St Mark's Building Fund.

A FESTIVAL OF SONGS at the Market House around 1910. The Barford St Martin Choral Society were performing when this picture was taken. They came in third.

ST MARK'S SCHOOLCHILDREN in Bourne Park to celebrate peace on Children's Day, 26 July 1919. Harold Whitworth took the picture with Miss Thomas standing far left holding a basket of goodies.

LATER ON, their teachers and parents joined them for tea. Miss Thomas is standing nearest the table and Mary, the daughter of Edward Charles Scott, is sitting on a lady's knee.

ST MARK'S SCHOOL SPORTS DAY, around 1910. Held in fields behind the Salisbury School, now Chafyn Grove. At least one boy or girl was proud of their daddy's performance that day.

A VIEW OF THE SPECTATORS. The chap standing to the left of the flag pole, wearing white trousers, is schoolteacher Edward Charles Scott. Boaters and panamas were clearly in fashion.

SUTTON'S BAKERY FOOTBALL TEAM just before the Great War. Frederick Sutton is in the centre, looking a little like Edward VII. Joseph James, Ball, Lear, McKewan and Shipsey were among the players.

THE WINNING TEAM. Fisherton House Tug of War Team beat St Pauls Conservative Club at a match held in September 1912. The victors floored their opponents in 9 seconds on the first pull and 54 on the second.

THE SALISBURY HARRIERS were in good spirits and quite undeterred by the rain at the start of a race with the Southampton team. The picture was taken near the Market House in about 1919.

MEMBERS OF THE SALISBURY CO-OPERATIVE SOCIETY at a fête held just before the Great War. Their banner has survived the years and is now in a private collection.

THE WOMEN'S SECTION of the Salisbury Co-operative Society on an outing to Breamore in June 1912. There's that motto again.

PARTICIPANTS OF THE PALESTINE EXHIBITION held at the Maundrel Hall in Fisherton Street around 1919. Miss Dorothy Sandford, sitting in the middle of the front row, later married Frederick James who is featured on page 110.

QUEEN MARY'S NEEDLEWORK GUILD in the Council Chamber during the Great War. The sewing party was photographed by Horace Messer.

THE GOLDEN AGE OF THE CHARABANC began in 1919. This party was setting off from Rawlings'
shop in Blue Boar Row in 1925. The 16-seater Maxwell was from the Sparrow & Vincent
fleet.

THE HIAWATHA & QUEEN COMPANY of Southampton made frequent trips to Salisbury. On this
occasion, in 1923, their passengers were office workers from Bevois Valley.

NOT ALL OUTINGS WERE BY CHARABANC as this 1920 picture shows. On Wednesdays and weekends the streets were full of motor carriages.

A WARMINSTER SUNDAY SCHOOL OUTING to Salisbury in 1925. The party was photographed in the Canal. It is interesting that the Burford vehicle, on the left, still had solid tyres.

WILLIAM (BILL) GARRETT, a Tenderfoot Scout of the 6th Salisbury, St Paul's Troop. His picture was taken at Futcher's studio around 1917.

AT VICTORIA PARK on 8 June 1910 hundreds of Wiltshire scouts took part in a display. The Codford Troop are seen using straw to demonstrate their mattress-making skills.

THE 1ST SALISBURY (YMCA) SCOUT TROOP at Reservoir Field camp, Harnham, in 1910. The father of Salisbury scouting, Percy James Southon, sits on the right, with arms folded. 'P.J.' as he was known, received his Scoutmaster's Warrant on 3 July 1909.

THE BLACKMORE MUSEUM was opened in 1867. This interior view of around 1890 clearly shows the fine oak hammer beam roof.

THE GIANT AND HOB NOB displayed in the Salisbury, South Wilts. and Blackmore Museum before 1930. The Giant's appearance has changed many times over the centuries so a visit to his present home, the Salisbury Museum at 65 The Close, is recommended if you would like to see how he looks today.

RIVERSIDE WALK around 1907, now known as Churchill Gardens. How often these days would you see a policeman taking a leisurely stroll through the pleasure gardens?

YOUNG LADIES PLAYING TENNIS at the Bishop's School in 1905. The goats may have been pets but certainly they were useful for keeping the grass down.

'WHAT DO YOU THINK OF BABY? SHE GOT FIRST PRIZE'. That is the message on the back of this photograph taken at the Harnham Flower Show on Bank Holiday 1908.

LATER THAT AFTERNOON sports were held and this picture shows a water polo team. Amateur photographer Charles Bridle is sitting on the ground, second from the right.

A SOLDIER AND HIS SWEETHEART starting out from West Harnham for a walk across Broken Bridges in 1906.

A VIEW OF BROKEN BRIDGES near Bemerton, 1907. The walk between Harnham and Bemerton was always very popular.

700TH ANNIVERSARY CELEBRATIONS in Salisbury, June 1927. Misses Horrell and Roper dressed in the style of 1830. They were photographed in the Close by F. Futcher.

W.J. PERRETT, R.A. GOURDIE, A.R. REID AND S.L. GRAY as four Salisbury City Peelers of around 1840. They were photographed when the procession stopped temporarily in Blue Boar Row.

THE WOMEN'S SECTION AND LOCAL RELIEF COMMITTEE of the British Legion entered two carts in the procession. They too were photographed as they made their way along Blue Boar Row.

THE FIRST RSPCA CART-HORSE PARADE, Whit Monday, 1908. The cart pictured here, near Fisherton Bridge, was entered by William Henry Baker of St Paul's Road. He received a special prize for the cart-horse which had been with one owner for the longest period.

ANOTHER WINNER. Frank Shergold, the Woodfalls carrier. Seen here with his van outside George Diffey's shop in St Thomas' Square after the 1911 Cart-horse Parade. He was awarded a special prize for the oldest carrier's horse.

SALISBURY PHOTOGRAPHERS

Arney, John and Son	43 Castle Street	1889–1890
(Victoria Studio)	29 Castle Street	1891–1896
Brooks, Harry	45 High Street	1897–1926
Brooks, Henry	60 High Street	1858–1917
Brooks, Mrs F.E.	60 High Street	1880–1926
Brown, Theodore	Portland House, Fisherton	1898–1902
	34a Castle Street	1903–1906
	3 Nelson Road	1904–1906
Buckle, Henry G.	3 Dews Road	1912–1921
Camera Corner	see J. Fowler Smith	
Collins (G) and Morgan	42 Rollestone Street	No dates recorded
Conduit Photographers	6 Bridge Street	1949–1953
	31 Devizes Road	1953–1959
Cosser, Whitfield & Co.	80 Castle Street	1905–1914
Dunmore, Alfred	Wilton Road	1875–1878
	117 Fisherton Street	1878–1880
	London Road	1880–1881
Eastman, Philip S.	29 Castle Street	1920–1953
Edwards, Thomas	30 St Ann Street	1864–1885
Ellis, W.T.	1 Dews Road	1920s
	Churchfields	1930s
Falcon Studios	4a Endless Street	1949–1953
Futcher, Frederick	19 Fisherton Street	1905–1988
(This company is still trading as F. Futcher and Son)		
Gearing, C.P.	High Street	1867–1868
Hall and Co.	2nd Floor, Midland Bank-Chambers, Market Place	1925–1926
Harding, Reginald.	see Royal Studios	
Henderson, James W.E.	79 Queen Alexandra Road	1931–1932
	35 St Andrew's Road	1932–1936

Jarvis, James E.	see Royal Central Photographic Co.	
Leman, E.	Queen Street.	1867–1868
	Fisherton Street	No dates recorded
Light, Herbert	79 Winchester Street	1913–1915
Macey, Mrs M.	2nd Floor, Midland Bank-Chambers, Market Place	1925–1932
Macey, E & N	140 Fisherton Street	1930–1938
Macy, Edwin	St Thomas' Square	1865–1880
Messer, Horace C.	29 Castle Street	1897–1920
Miell, James Wesley	21 Catherine Street	1859–1867
	45 Catherine Street	1867–1880
	Fisherton Street	1880–1885
	St John's Street	1885–1897
Mortimer, Miss Ivy B.M.	2nd Floor, Midland Bank-Chambers, Market Place	1923–1927
Martin, Muir Jnr.	37 Blue Boar Row	1944–1959
Mullins, Bertram S.	80 Castle Street	1915–1923
Neville	High Street	1865–1866
Owen, James	29 Catherine Street	1878–1896
Owen, Mrs F.	29 Catherine Street	1896–1903
Photokraft	112 Fisherton Street	1942–1959
Pitcher, William Thomas	St Ann Street	1859–1860
Rewse, Harry Marlow	133 Fisherton Street	1890–1896
	163a Fisherton Street	1896–1898
	131 South Western Road	1898–1906
	25 Water Lane	1906–1930
Ritchie,	Not known.	1920s.
Roberts, B.E.W.	23 High Street	1950–1953
Rogers, Edmund	De Vaux Place.	1865–1879
Rogers, Mary Ann	De Vaux Place.	1879–1905
Royal Central Photo. Co. (Manager, James E. Jarvis)	38 High Street	1903–1919
Royal Studios (Manager, Reginald W. Harding)	38 High Street	1919–1939
Sands, George, F.	45 Canal	1911–1915
Sanger, Edward Wynne	Devizes Road	1878–1885
Scotford Ltd.	6 Queen Street	1920–1923
Smith, Fowler. (Camera Corner)	16 Winchester Street	1931–1936
Smith, J. Fowler	44 Blue Boar Row	1936–1940
	47 Catherine Street	1940–1944

	45 Canal	1944–1953
	23 High Street	1953–1959
Sutton, Stanley	45 Canal	1919–1944
Targett, Edward John	79 Winchester Street	1878–1880
	45 Catherine Street	1880–1886
	79 Winchester Street	1886–1912
Taylor, Charles	Wilton Road	1865–1866
Treble, Frederick	14 Catherine Street	1861–1867
	High Street	1867–1868
Turner, Charles	83 Castle Street	1903–1904
Whitworth, Harold	3a St Ann Street	1919–1920
	49 New Street	1920–1931
	15 Meadow Road	1931–1950
Witcomb, Charles John	Milford Street	1862–1867
Witcomb, Charles J and Son	47 Catherine Street	1867–1872
(The son was Sydney George)	10 Catherine Street	1872–1886
	8/10 Catherine Street	1886–1908
Witcomb, Frank Sydney	53 Canal	1920–1925
	16a Catherine Street	1926–1942

Portraits Painted
Artistic Photographs
& Enlargements
Arney & Son
Victoria Studio
·29·
Castle Street
SALISBURY

COPIES OR ENLARGEMENTS,
ANY SIZE TO ORDER.

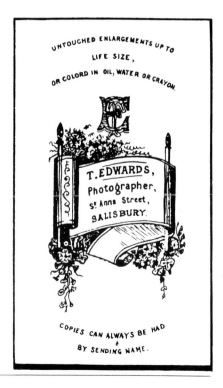

UNTOUCHED ENLARGEMENTS UP TO
LIFE SIZE,
OR COLORD IN OIL, WATER OR CRAYON.

T. EDWARDS,
Photographer,
St Anns Street,
SALISBURY.

COPIES CAN ALWAYS BE HAD
BY SENDING NAME.

ACKNOWLEDGEMENTS

My thanks go to many people who willingly helped with my research over the past few months. I have endeavoured to name them all but if anyone has been forgotten the fault is mine and I do hope that my apologies will be accepted.

In particular I am grateful to Mr Peter Saunders, the author of the first volume of *Salisbury in Old Photographs*, for letting me compile this second selection. He encouraged and guided me from the outset and when I needed advice, he gave it.

Ann and Geoffrey Crowe read the captions and suggested ways to improve them, their contribution was much appreciated.

I am also indebted to the following individuals and organisations who gave permission for their photographs to be reproduced or for helping in various other ways:

Mr Bill Garratt and Mr Frederick James for sharing their years of knowledge and experience and for providing photographs from their personal collections.

Castle Cameras; for donating the photographic paper from which the prints were made.

Salisbury's leading postcard and photograph collectors; Miss Pat Blake, Mr Keith Chapman, Mr David Smith, Mr Jim Smith and Mr David Ward. Thanks to them for allowing me to copy and reproduce pictures. We should all be grateful that they are preserving our city's photographic heritage.

Salisbury Museum; Mr Peter Saunders, the Curator and Miss Clare Conibere, Assistant Curator (Archaeology) for giving me access to the museum library and photographic collection. A number of their prints are reproduced within.

Salisbury Reference Library; Mr Edward Boyle, Miss Gillian Roberts and Mrs Carol Hausner. Their microfilmed copies of *The Salisbury Times* were used to date the pictures in the 'Events' section.

The Salisbury Journal; Mr Gareth Weekes, the Editor, for allowing me to view old copies of his newspaper, for giving publicity and permitting me to use copyright photographs.

The Salisbury Times; Miss Jennifer Rogers, for giving publicity and to the readers who, through the 'Puzzle Picture' feature, have identified many of the photographs.

Wiltshire Record Office; Mr Ken Rogers for allowing me to reproduce photographs and to the Archivists, Search Room Assistants and Strong Room Assistants who are always so helpful and friendly.

Mrs Mary Abernethy; Mr Nick Baldwin; Miss Mary Bridle; Mrs Q. Burt; Mrs Joyce Burton; Mrs Pat Charles; Miss E.N. Crouch; F. Futcher & Son; Gibbs, Mew & Company; Mr Doug Goodman; Mr Len Goodyear; Miss E.M. Harris; Mr Ron Kerley; Mr Robert Key MP; Mr Tony Martin; Mrs Kathleen Maton; Mr Albert Noyce; Mr Ken Phillips; Miss Barbara Pinniger; Mr R. Pritchett; Mr H.B. Radcliffe; Mrs Dorothy Roberts; Mrs Margaret Sanger; Mrs Iris Smith; Mr E.H.J. Southon; Mrs Mary Topp; Mr Stanley Witcomb and Mr Douglas Young.